ANTIETAM EXPEDITION GUIDE

A comprehensive guide to the Battle of Antietam

Travel adventures that leave you smarter!

The Antietam Expedition Guide is a unique combination of a computer DVD-ROM, a self-guide audio tour, and an illustrated guidebook, designed to take you on an unforgettable journey to the hallowed grounds of the Antietam National Battlefield.

Special thanks to John Howard, Keith Snyder, Ted Alexander and the staff at Antietam National Battlefield Park.

Disclaimer

This book is intended for viewing at tour stops only. Please keep your eyes on the road at all times while driving. TravelBrains shall have neither liability nor responsibility to any person or entity with respect to any loss or damage caused, or alleged to have been caused, directly or indirectly, by the use of this product.

ANTIETAM BATTLEFIELD TOUR

"In the time that I am writing, every stalk of corn in the northern and greater part of the field was cut as closely as could have been done with a knife, and the slain lay in rows precisely as they had stood in their ranks a few moments before. It was never my fortune to witness a more bloody, dismal battlefield."

UNION MAJOR GENERAL JOSEPH HOOKER
I CORPS COMMANDER
ARMY OF THE POTOMAC

CONTENTS

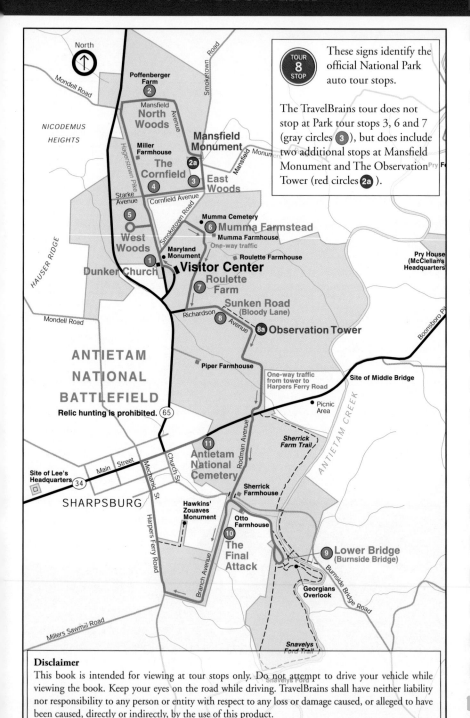

These signs identify the official National Park auto tour stops.

The TravelBrains tour does not stop at Park tour stops 3, 6 and 7 (gray circles ③), but does include two additional stops at Mansfield Monument and The Observation Tower (red circles ②a).

North

Mondell Road

Poffenberger Farm ②

Smoketown Road

NICODEMUS HEIGHTS

Mansfield Avenue

North Woods

Mansfield Monument

Mansfield Monument

Pry F

Miller Farmhouse

The Cornfield ④

②a ③

East Woods

HAGERSTOWN PIKE

Starke Avenue

Cornfield Avenue

⑤

West Woods

Smoketown Road

Mumma Cemetery

⑥ Mumma Farmstead

Mumma Farmhouse

One-way traffic

Pry House (McClellan's Headquarters)

Maryland Monument

Roulette Farmhouse

① Dunker Church

Visitor Center

⑦ Roulette Farm

HAUSER RIDGE

Mondell Road

Richardson Avenue

⑧ Sunken Road (Bloody Lane)

⑧a Observation Tower

Boonsboro Pk

ANTIETAM NATIONAL BATTLEFIELD

Piper Farmhouse

One-way traffic from tower to Harpers Ferry Road

Site of Middle Bridge

Relic hunting is prohibited. ⑥⑤

Picnic Area

ANTIETAM CREEK

Rodman Avenue

Sherrick Farm Trail

Site of Lee's Headquarters ③④

Main Street

Mechanic St

Church St

⑪ Antietam National Cemetery

SHARPSBURG

Harpers Ferry Road

Sherrick Farmhouse

Hawkins' Zouaves Monument

Otto Farmhouse

⑩ The Final Attack

Branch Avenue

⑨ Lower Bridge (Burnside Bridge)

Burnside Bridge Road

Georgians Overlook

Millers Sawmill Road

Snavelys Ford Trail

Disclaimer

This book is intended for viewing at tour stops only. Do not attempt to drive your vehicle while viewing the book. Keep your eyes on the road while driving. TravelBrains shall have neither liability nor responsibility to any person or entity with respect to any loss or damage caused, or alleged to have been caused, directly or indirectly, by the use of this product.

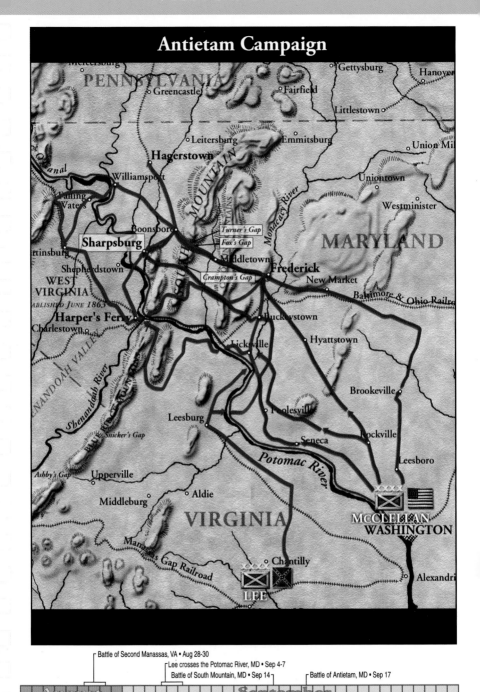

Antietam Campaign

Battle of Second Manassas, VA • Aug 28-30
Lee crosses the Potomac River, MD • Sep 4-7
Battle of South Mountain, MD • Sep 14
Battle of Antietam, MD • Sep 17

August										September																											
23	24	25	26	27	28	29	30	31	1	2	3	4	5	6	7	8	9	10	11	12	13	14	15	16	17	18	19	20	21	22	23	24	25	26	27	28	29	30

Confederates enter Frederick, MD • Sep 6
Lee divides his army • Sep 10
McClellan reaches Frederick, MD • Sep 12
Jackson attacks Harper's Ferry, VA • Sep 12-15

3

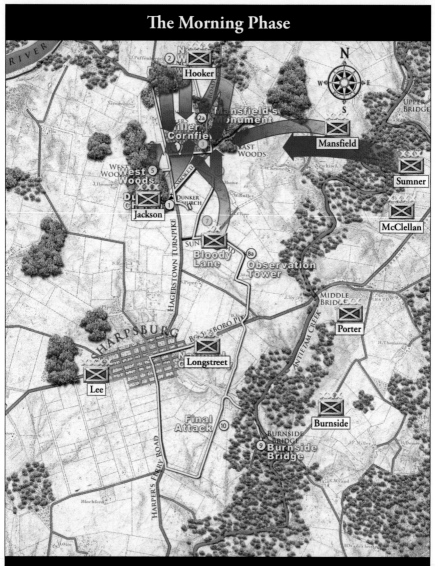

The Morning Phase

Hooker

Mansfield's Monument

Mansfield

Miller Cornfield

East Woods

Sumner

West Woods

McClellan

Dunker Church

Jackson

Bloody Lane

Observation Tower

Middle Bridge

Porter

HARPSBURG

Longstreet

Lee

Burnside

Final Attack

Burnside Bridge

Approximately 6:00 A.M to 9:00 A.M.

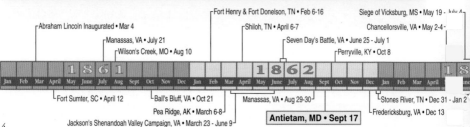

Abraham Lincoln Inaugurated • Mar 4

Fort Henry & Fort Donelson, TN • Feb 6-16

Siege of Vicksburg, MS • May 19 - July 4

Shiloh, TN • April 6-7

Chancellorsville, VA • May 2-4

Manassas, VA • July 21

Seven Day's Battle, VA • June 25 - July 1

Wilson's Creek, MO • Aug 10

Perryville, KY • Oct 8

1861

1862

18

Jan Feb Mar April May June July Aug Sept Oct Nov Dec | Jan Feb Mar April May June July Aug Sept Oct Nov Dec | Jan Feb Mar April | ne

Fort Sumter, SC • April 12

Ball's Bluff, VA • Oct 21

Manassas, VA • Aug 29-30

Stones River, TN • Dec 31 - Jan 2

Pea Ridge, AK • March 6-8

Fredericksburg, VA • Dec 13

Jackson's Shenandoah Valley Campaign, VA • March 23 - June 9

Antietam, MD • Sept 17

The Midday Phase

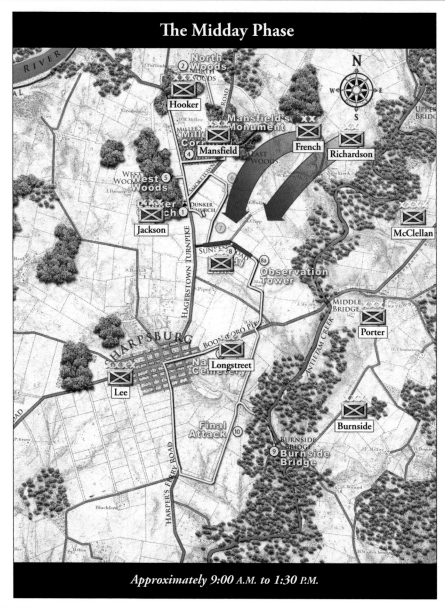

Approximately 9:00 A.M. to 1:30 P.M.

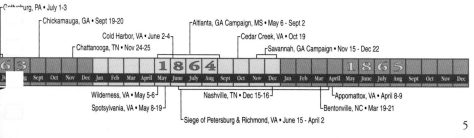

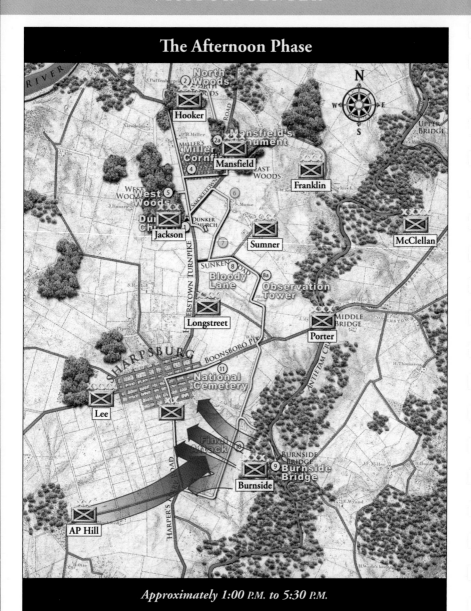

The Afternoon Phase

Approximately 1:00 P.M. to 5:30 P.M.

Did you know?

The Dunker Church was used as an embalming station after the battle. Although the concepts of embalming date back to ancient Egypt, the practice was not in wide spread use in America until the Civil War. The preservation process involved the insertion of a rubber tube into an artery under the armpit, through which a preservative like arsenic was pumped. Formaldehyde had not yet been discovered. Since the process could cost up to $100, it was most commonly performed on the bodies of officers.

Army of the Potomac

  Total Strength:
85,000 troops
300 Cannons

McClellan

I Corps	II Corps	V Corps
Hooker	Sumner	Porter
VI Corps	IX Corps	XII Corps
Franklin	Burnside	Mansfield

Cavalry
Division

Pleasonton

Order of Battle

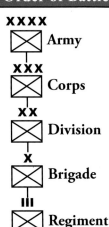

xxxx ⊠ **Army**

xxx ⊠ **Corps**

xx ⊠ **Division**

x ⊠ **Brigade**

||| ⊠ **Regiment**

These symbols are used on the battlefield maps in this book to denote the general locations of troops.

Military Symbols

⊠	◨	●
Infantry	**Cavalry**	**Artillery**

Army of Northern Virginia

  Total Strength:
40,000 troops
200 Cannons

Lee

Cavalry

Longstreet's Wing	Jackson's Wing	Stuart

Note: Confederate Corps were usually named after their commanders.

Did you know?

Nearly every major battle of the Civil War was fought by West Point graduates commanding the armies of both sides. McClellan (1846) and Lee (1829) both graduated 2nd in their respective West Point classes. McClellan was 35 years old in September 1862, 20 years younger than Lee.

Bloodiest Battles of the Civil War

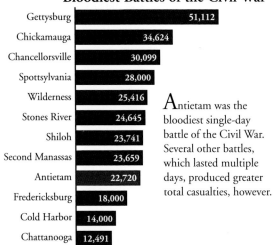

Battle	Casualties
Gettysburg	51,112
Chickamauga	34,624
Chancellorsville	30,099
Spottsylvania	28,000
Wilderness	25,416
Stones River	24,645
Shiloh	23,741
Second Manassas	23,659
Antietam	22,720
Fredericksburg	18,000
Cold Harbor	14,000
Chattanooga	12,491
First Manassas	4,122

Casualties

Antietam was the bloodiest single-day battle of the Civil War. Several other battles, which lasted multiple days, produced greater total casualties, however.

7

Guide to Battlefield Markers & Monuments

War Department Tablets

In the 1890s, the War Department placed over 300 tablets around the battlefield to mark the locations of the armies. Each tablet provides detailed information about the participants that were located near each respective tablet and the action that occurred there.

Mortuary Cannons

Upside down cannon barrels, mounted in blocks of stone, signify the approximate locations where six generals were killed or mortally wounded during the battle: three Confederate and three Union.

Confederate Generals	Union Generals
William E. Starke	Joseph K. F. Mansfield
George B. Anderson	Israel Richardson
Lawrence O'Bryan Branch	Isaac Peace Rodman

Artillery Locations

The Union and Confederate armies brought over 500 cannons with them to the Battle at Antietam. The cannons on the battlefield today, mark the locations of significant artillery formations at the time of the battle. The cannon barrels are authentic Civil War guns, but the wheels and carriages are reconstructions.

Monuments

There are over 100 monuments on the battlefield today. Typically located close to where the troops fought during the battle, the monuments were placed by veterans and states to commemorate the sacrifices of the soldiers. The majority of the monuments are Union, primarily because the former soldiers of the Confederacy could not afford to build monuments following the ravages of the war.

National Park Service Waysides

Located at each of the auto tour stops, these information signs provide maps, photographs and quotes that help explain the story of Antietam.

H elp the Park...

Adopt-a-Monument is a great way to help the National Park Service maintain more than 100 monuments and memorials at Antietam. If you or your organization is interested, please visit http://www.nps.gov/anti/supportyourpark/adopt-a-monument.htm

Traveling with children?

Here are some activities to keep the whole family involved.

The Great TravelBrains Photo Scavenger Hunt

At many of the tour stops you will find a photo scavenger hunt item to find. These picture taking opportunities let you capture the places and monuments that are essential to telling your Antietam battlefield story. When you return home, be sure to visit the TravelBrains web site (www.TravelBrains.com) to download and print your own personal Antietam photo album. It includes famous historic images next to blank spaces for your modern photographs, allowing you to compare the past with the present.

TOUR 1 STOP Stand in the same location where this historic photograph of Dunker Church was made and take your own modern day picture. See page 11 for a larger version of the photograph.

TOUR 2 STOP Take a picture of your family in front of the Clara Barton Monument.

TOUR 4 STOP Find the Texas State Monument and take a picture in front of it.

TOUR 8 STOP Explore the Sunken Road and take a picture in the location where the 2nd North Carolina Infantry Regiment fought.

TOUR 8a STOP Take a picture in front of the Irish Brigade monument.

Irish Brigade

TOUR 9 STOP Take a picture of your family in front of Burnside Bridge and next to the 51st Pennsylvania Infantry monument.

TOUR 11 STOP Take a picture of Captain Von Bachelle's grave. To find the grave, walk directly to the U.S. Soldier monument in the middle of the cemetery, turn 180 degrees around to face the entrance and look at the first row of headstones to the right of the pathway. Von Bachelle's stone is the seventh to the right.

THE GREAT TRAVELBRAINS TRIVIA CHALLENGE

Easy

1. Who commanded the Union army at Antietam?

A. Joseph Hooker
B. Ambrose Burnside
C. George McClellan

2. Southerners refer to the Battle of Antietam by what name?

A. The Battle of Sharpsburg
B. The Battle of Bloody Lane
C. The Battle of The Cornfield

3. Antietam is the name of what feature near the battlefield?

A. Church
B. Town
C. Creek

4. What was General George B. McClellan's nickname?

A. Little Mac
B. Big Mac
C. Whopper

5. Antietam holds what distinction in the course of the Civil War?

A. The bloodiest battle
B. The bloodiest day
C. The northern most battle

6. What was the name of the standard rifle bullet used by Civil War soldiers?

A. Round shot
B. Buckeye ball
C. Minié Ball

7. Which Union General's distinctive facial hair was the source of the term sideburns?

A. Winfield Scott Hancock
B. Ambrose Burnside
C. Benjamin Butler

Expert

1. Which of these commanders was Stonewall Jackson's brother-in-law?

A. D.H. Hill
B. James Longstreet
C. William Tecumseh Sherman

2. Which General designed a horse saddle that became standard issue for the cavalry up until 1942?

A. J.E.B. Stuart
B. Alfred Pleasonton
C. George McClellan

3. The Union surrender at Harper's Ferry on September 15, 1862 stood as the largest capitulation of Federal forces in U.S. history until when?

A. Appomattox, 1865
B. Bataan, Philippines, 1942
C. Bastogne, France 1944

4. Legend has it that the nickname "Iron Brigade" was bestowed on the men of Gibbon's brigade following which battle?

A. Antietam
B. Second Manassas
C. South Mountain

5. What did Union General Burnside invent?

A. Card game
B. Shaver
C. Carbine rifle

6. Future Presidents Rutherford B. Hayes and William McKinley were both members of which regiment?

A. 23rd Ohio
B. 6th Wisconsin
C. 19th Indiana

7. What was the popular name for the 9th New York Infantry Regiment?

A. The Bucktails
B. Hawkin's Zouaves
C. The Excelsior Brigade

Easy Answers: C A C A B C B
Expert Answers: A C B C C A B

Col. Stephen D. Lee

"Sharpsburg was artillery Hell."

Describing the intense counter-battery fire his men received at Antietam, Confederate artillerist, Colonel Stephen D. Lee wrote, "Pray that you may never see another Sharpsburg. Sharpsburg was artillery Hell." On the morning of September 17, S.D. Lee's artillery line was placed on the high ground adjacent to the Dunker Church. The caisson, visible in the image below, probably belonged to his battalion. S.D. Lee was not related to General Robert E. Lee. However, Robert E. Lee did have a son who served in the artillery and fought at Antietam. Lee's youngest son, Robert E. Lee, Jr., was a member of the Rockbridge Artillery. At one point during the day, Robert Jr. approached his father and asked him if he was going to send him back into battle. Lee replied, "Yes, my son, you all must do what you can to help drive these people back."

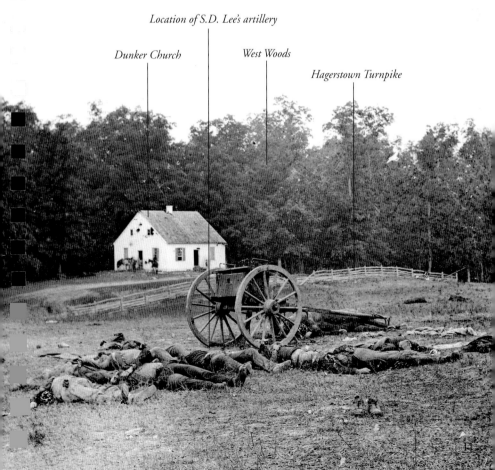

Location of S.D. Lee's artillery

Dunker Church

West Woods

Hagerstown Turnpike

Artillery of the Civil War

CASE SHOT

Case shot, sometimes called shrapnel, was a hollow iron shell (round or elongated) filled with round balls and sealed in melted rosin or sulphur. A powder charge in the core of the shell was ignited by a timed fuse. When the shell exploded, the balls and twisted fragments of iron tore through soldiers and horses.

SHELL

A shell was a cast iron projectile (round or elongated) filled with black powder. Artillerists could choose an impact fuse or time fuse to explode the shell. An impact fuse exploded when it hit a target. A time fuse was ignited by the discharge of the cannon and exploded at a set time after ignition. Experienced artillerists could accurately time the fuse to explode the shell over the target.

CANISTER

Canister was a tin can filled with iron balls (a little smaller than the size of golf balls) packed in sawdust. This type of ammunition effectively turned the cannon into a large shotgun. It was used at close range against infantry. In extreme cases, double and triple canister rounds were packed into the cannon muzzle and fired.

SOLID SHOT

Solid Shot was a round ball or elongated projectile made of solid iron. It was typically used at longer ranges against massed troops, fortifications, and enemy batteries. Solid shot (or bolts as they were sometimes called when fired from rifled cannon) were not designed to explode.

THE ARTILLERY CREW

A well-drilled crew could load and fire a cannon about three times per minute. A gun crew of ten men was ideal. A lieutenant and a sergeant gave orders; a gunner aimed the cannon; and the remaining seven crew members, each identified with a number, cleaned, loaded and fired the cannon.

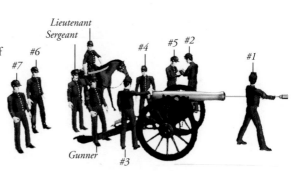

0 yds.

12-Pounder Napoleon

This famous cannon was named after Emperor Napoleon III of France. The term "12-Pounder" comes from the twelve-pound artillery round it fired. By the end of the Civil War it was by far the most widely used artillery piece in both armies. It had an effective range of one mile and could fire solid shot, shell, case shot and canister rounds. Made of bronze, the tube turns green as it oxidizes over time.

range 1 mi

10-Pounder Parrott Rifle

provided spin

Made of cast iron with a wrought iron jacket, this cannon was named for its designer, Robert Parrott of the West Point Foundry. Cast iron guns were better at maintaining the rifle grooves on the inside of the tubes (bronze was too soft), but they were brittle and could crack or explode on discharge. Parrott devised a solution to this problem by wrapping a hot band of iron around the breech, or base, of the tube.

↑ accuracy

3-Inch Ordnance Rifle

Made entirely of wrought iron, the 3-inch ordnance rifle was expensive and time consuming to produce. Its durability and accuracy, however, made it a favorite among artillerists on both sides of the war. The name of the cannon is derived from the diameter of the gun's bore, a standard nomenclature practice for rifled cannon. Smoothbore cannon, on the other hand, are typically referenced by the weight of the solid shot they fire.

2,000- 3000 yards
Practical Range

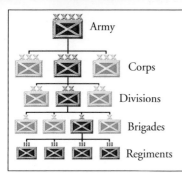

The Regiment

Regiments were the tactical fighting unit of the Civil War. According to regulations, a volunteer infantry regiment was supposed to consist of 1,000 men organized into 10 companies of 100 men each. In reality, however, the average regimental strength was substantially less. By 1863, the average Union regiment mustered fewer than 400 men.

Army

Corps

Divisions

Brigades

Regiments

Regimental Battle Formation

Two Ranks Deep

In combat, regiments deployed in long straight lines two rows (ranks) deep.

Staff

Colonel
Regiment's
Commander

Lt. Colonel

Band

Major

Adjutant

Sgt. Major

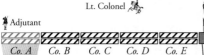

| Co. A | Co. B | Co. C | Co. D | Co. E | Co. F | Co. G | Co. H | Co. J | Co. K |

Skirmishers

Two companies were often sent out in front as skirmishers to probe the enemy's lines.

The Colors

Regiments carried their flags or "colors" in the center of the battle line. They were instrumental in guiding the regiment when the din of battle made verbal commands difficult to hear.

Smoothbore musket effective range: 100 yds.

Changing Technology

The American Civil War marked the first time in the history of warfare that rifle muskets were used in such large numbers. This weapon nearly quadrupled the effective killing range of an infantryman to nearly 400 yards under ideal circumstances. The rifle-musket achieved this astounding accuracy by etching grooves on the inside of the gun barrel. When the gun was fired, the grooves caused the bullet to spiral in flight, giving it more stability, range and accuracy.

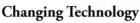

50 yds.

Civil War Tactics

At the time, the French military was considered to be on the leading edge of strategic and tactical theory. French tactics relied heavily on offensive force by large masses of troops. Flanking movements and frontal assaults were the primary tactics of choice.

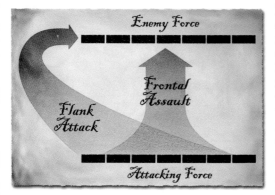

FLANKING MOVEMENTS relied on speed and maneuverability to achieve results. Passing around the end of an enemy line, the attacker would bring his troops to bear on the opponent's flank, or end. One of the advantages to flanking the enemy was the ability to fire into the sides of the enemy line. This type of fire, also known as enfilade was very effective.

THE FRONTAL ASSAULT held the allure of a quick and decisive victory. Using this tactic, troops were massed and sent head long at the enemy. Massing large numbers of men ensured that enough of the troops would arrive at the focal point of the attack to overwhelm the enemy and drive them from the field.

Many of the generals who faced each other during the Civil War witnessed this tactic achieve great success during the Mexican War, just fifteen years prior. The experience would have a lasting impact on these officers. Even though advances in firearms and cannon technology had given the advantage to the defender, many generals would continue to employ this tactic during the Civil War.

en·fi·lade (enfə-lād')

n. Gunfire directed along the length of a target, such as a column of troops.

v. tr. To rake with gunfire.

Rifle musket effective range: 200 - 400 yards

(actual size)

Minié Ball

The Minié Ball was named after French army officer Claude-Etienne Minié. Upon firing, the base of the bullet would expand in the barrel forcing it against the rifle grooves that lined the tube. The grooves, in turn, caused the bullet to spin, which greatly improved its flight characteristics.

Minié Ball Cartridge

— *Minié Ball*

— *Wooden Plug*
— *Gunpowder*

— *Paper Shell*

---

100 yds.   150 yds.   200 yds.

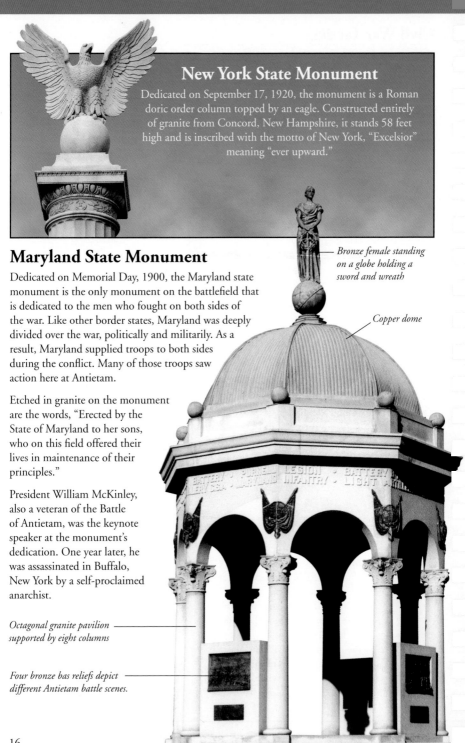

New York State Monument

Dedicated on September 17, 1920, the monument is a Roman doric order column topped by an eagle. Constructed entirely of granite from Concord, New Hampshire, it stands 58 feet high and is inscribed with the motto of New York, "Excelsior" meaning "ever upward."

Maryland State Monument

Dedicated on Memorial Day, 1900, the Maryland state monument is the only monument on the battlefield that is dedicated to the men who fought on both sides of the war. Like other border states, Maryland was deeply divided over the war, politically and militarily. As a result, Maryland supplied troops to both sides during the conflict. Many of those troops saw action here at Antietam.

Etched in granite on the monument are the words, "Erected by the State of Maryland to her sons, who on this field offered their lives in maintenance of their principles."

President William McKinley, also a veteran of the Battle of Antietam, was the keynote speaker at the monument's dedication. One year later, he was assassinated in Buffalo, New York by a self-proclaimed anarchist.

Bronze female standing on a globe holding a sword and wreath

Copper dome

Octagonal granite pavilion supported by eight columns

Four bronze bas reliefs depict different Antietam battle scenes.

16

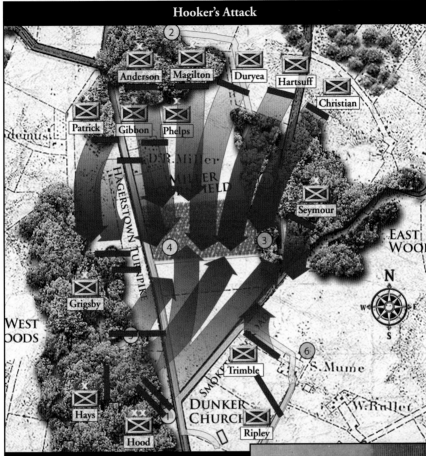

Hooker's Attack

Approximately 6:00 A.M. to 8:00 A.M.

Did you know?

General Hooker acquired his nickname as a result of a journalistic blunder. In 1862 a news headline describing the fighting on the Virginia Peninsula was supposed to have read, "Fighting - Joe Hooker." But when the story went to print, the dash was inadvertently left out. Thereafter, the general was known as, "Fighting Joe Hooker."

In 1863 Hooker was given command of the Army of the Potomac, but led it in a disastrous defeat at Chancellorsville. Hooker's most lasting contribution to the army was his decision to issue corps badges to the infantry. Each corps was assigned its own unique symbol, which became a source of pride with the troops.

Maj. Gen. Joseph Hooker

Civil War Medicine

It was said that the Civil War was fought at the end of the medical Middle Ages. Indeed, it was a sorry state of affairs for a soldier who was injured or fell ill. Very little was known about germs or disease and the concepts of sanitary practice were still years away. Additionally, advances in weapon technology and the

Portable Drug Kit

introduction of the Minié ball were producing more lethal and complicated battlefield injuries. At the same time, general hospitals to treat the thousands of injured and sick did not exist at the outbreak of the war. Surgeons too were woefully unprepared. Few of them had attended medical school for more than two years and even fewer had ever performed surgery prior to their first battlefield amputations. On the job training was not hard to find, however. Soon soldiers were calling the surgeons, "Sawbones," for all the limbs they were sawing off.

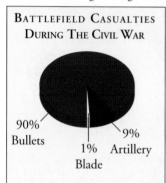

BATTLEFIELD CASUALTIES DURING THE CIVIL WAR

90% Bullets
1% Blade
9% Artillery

The soldier's deadliest enemy, however, was disease. For every one soldier that died from battle wounds, two died from disease. Overcrowded and unsanitary camp conditions, poor screening of new recruits and outbreaks of measles, malaria and other diseases were all contributors. The most common ailment suffered by the common soldier was dysentery, an inflammation of the bowel, usually caused by bacteria or parasites that resulted in pain, fever, and severe diarrhea, often accompanied by blood. More men died of diarrhea and dysentery than were killed on all the battlefields of the Civil War. The typical treatment for the "Tennessee Trots" was opium because it caused the bowels to stop moving.

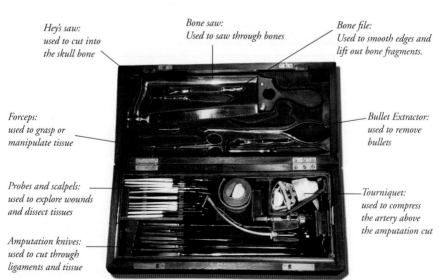

Hey's saw:
used to cut into the skull bone

Bone saw:
Used to saw through bones

Bone file:
Used to smooth edges and lift out bone fragments.

Forceps:
used to grasp or manipulate tissue

Bullet Extractor:
used to remove bullets

Probes and scalpels:
used to explore wounds and dissect tissues

Tourniquet:
used to compress the artery above the amputation cut

Amputation knives:
used to cut through ligaments and tissue

Surgeon's kit

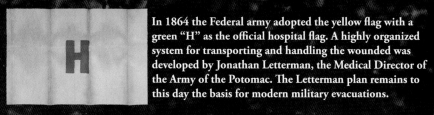

In 1864 the Federal army adopted the yellow flag with a green "H" as the official hospital flag. A highly organized system for transporting and handling the wounded was developed by Jonathan Letterman, the Medical Director of the Army of the Potomac. The Letterman plan remains to this day the basis for modern military evacuations.

Did you know?

Union Dr. Edward Revere, the grandson of Revolutionary patriot Paul Revere, was killed at the Battle of Antietam. He was a physician with the 20th Massachusetts.

Union surgeon performing an amputation

Clara Barton

"*A man lying upon the ground asked for drink. I stooped to give it, and having raised him with my right hand, was holding the cup to his lips with my left, when I felt a sudden twitch of the loose sleeve of my dress, the poor fellow sprang from my hands and fell back quivering, in the agonies of death. A ball had passed between my body and the right arm which supported him — cutting through the sleeve, and passing through his chest from shoulder to shoulder.*"

- Clara Barton

Maj. Gen. Joseph K.F. Mansfield

General Mansfield's career as a field commander lasted just two days. He was mortally wounded while attempting to deploy his troops near the East Woods. The mortuary cannon, located on Mansfield Monument Road, marks the general vicinity of his wounding.

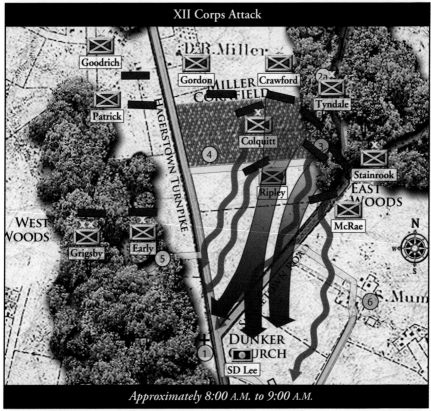

XII Corps Attack

Approximately 8:00 A.M. to 9:00 A.M.

After command of the XII Corps passed from Mansfield to Williams, Brigadier General George Greene spearheaded an attack that drove the Confederates back to the Dunker Church.

Brig. Gen. Alpheus S. Williams

Brig. Gen. George S. Greene

"As we appeared at the edge of the corn, a long line of men in butternut and gray rose up from the ground. Simultaneously, the hostile battle lines opened a tremendous fire upon each other. Men, I can not say fell; they were knocked out of the ranks by dozens. But we jumped over the fence, and pushed on, loading, firing, and shouting as we advanced. There was, on the part of the men, great hysterical excitement, eagerness to go forward, and a reckless disregard of life, of everything but victory."

- Major Rufus R. Dawes

Through the Cornfield courtesy Keith Rocco

The Iron Brigade

Brig. Gen. John Gibbon

The Iron Brigade was originally dubbed the "Black Hat Brigade" because of the distinctive headgear they wore. Instead of wearing the typical Kepi cap, they chose to wear the regular army dress hat called the "Hardee hat." The hat was also sometimes called the "Jeff Davis hat" because it was introduced to the military during Jefferson Davis' tenure as the United States Secretary of War. The Hardee hat was pinned up on one side with a brass eagle. The brass bugle on the hat above identifies the wearer as a member of the infantry. Image courtesy of Dirty Billy's Hats.

Company I, 7th Wisconsin Volunteer Infantry Regiment of the Iron Brigade.

Hood's Texas Brigade

Brig. Gen. John B. Hood

Eight color bearers were shot down trying to protect the colors of the 1st Texas Volunteer Infantry Regiment. Lost on the battlefield, the flag was picked up by a Pennsylvania soldier from amongst the dead. The "Lone Star" flag was made from the wedding dress of Mrs. L. T. Wigfall, whose husband, formerly Senator Wigfall, had been colonel of the 1st Texas.

Youngest full general
Lost leg
Paralyzed arm

82% casualty
8 color-bearers
shot down

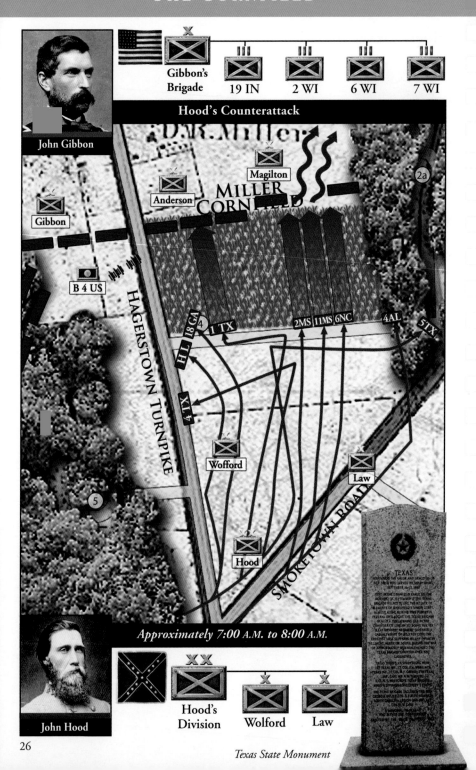

John Gibbon

Gibbon's Brigade
19 IN
2 WI
6 WI
7 WI

Hood's Counterattack

D.R. Miller

Magilton

Anderson

MILLER CORNFIELD

Gibbon

B 4 US

2a

HAGERSTOWN TURNPIKE

HL 18 GA 4

1 TX

2MS 11MS 6NC

4AL

5 TX

4 TX

Wofford

Law

5

SMOKETOWN ROAD

Hood

Approximately 7:00 A.M. to 8:00 A.M.

Hood's Division
Wolford
Law

John Hood

26

Texas State Monument

TEXAS

"We were then in the vortex of the battle."

John Cook enlisted in the army at the age of thirteen. Recalling the events at Antietam, Cook said, "...seeing the cannoneers nearly all down, and one, with a pouch full of ammunition, lying dead, I unstrapped the pouch, started for the battery and worked as a cannoneer. We were then in the vortex of the battle. The enemy had made three desperate attempts to capture us, the last time coming within ten or fifteen feet of our guns. It was at this time that General Gibbon, seeing the condition of the battery, came to the gun that stood in the pike, and in full uniform of a brigadier-general, worked as a gunner and cannoneer. He was very conspicuous, and it is indeed surprising, that he came away alive."

Bugler John Cook

Captain Werner Von Bachelle, commander of company F of the 6th Wisconsin had a pet Newfoundland dog that was his constant companion. Von Bachelle had taught the dog to do military salutes and other tricks that entertained the men of his company. When Von Bachelle was mortally wounded along the Hagerstown Pike on September 17, the dog remained by his master's side. Following the battle, survivors of the 6th Wisconsin returned to the area and discovered the lifeless dog laying atop his master's body. In tribute to the fallen commander, they buried Von Bachelle with his faithful companion.

Cpt. Werner Von Bachelle

Newfoundland Dog
representational image

Monument to the 84th New York (also known as the 14th Brooklyn)

This Alexander Gardner photograph, taken along the west side of the Hagerstown Pike, shows the bodies of Confederate soldiers. Most of the men were likely from General William E. Starke's Louisiana Brigade. During the morning phase of the battle, Starke's men wheeled east to form a line of battle along the fence. From this location they exchanged fire with men from the 6th Wisconsin some fifty yards away.

Miller farm lane

The Hagerstown Pike can be seen running approximately north and south between the post-and-rail fence that bordered the road.

The Miller Cornfield was located east of the pike, approximately 250 yards north of the spot where this photograph was taken.

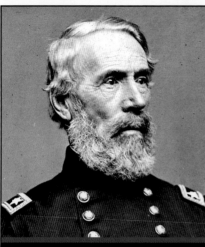

Maj. Gen. Edwin V. Sumner

Maj. Gen. John Sedgwick

Lee's Counterattack in the West Woods

Approximately 9:30 A.M. to 10:30 A.M.

Cpt. Oliver Wendell Holmes Jr.

HERE, SEPT. 17TH, 1862, THE FIFTEENTH REG. MASS. VOLUNTEERS, WITH THE FIRST COMPANY ANDREW SHARPSHOOTERS ATTACHED, 606 MEN OF ALL RANKS, COMMANDED BY LIEUT. COL. JOHN W. KIMBALL, GORMAN'S BRIGADE, SEDGWICK'S DIVISION, SECOND ARMY CORPS, MET AND ENGAGED THEREON BY THE BRIGADES OF BARKSDALE, EARLY AND BRANSCALE. WITHIN THIRTY MINUTES 330 MEN FELLING, 75 KILLED AND 255 WOUNDED. 43 TOTAL OF WOUNDS.

15TH REG. MASS. VOLS.

Men of the 15th Massachusetts Volunteers Infantry Regiment were recruited mainly from Worcester, Massachusetts.

31

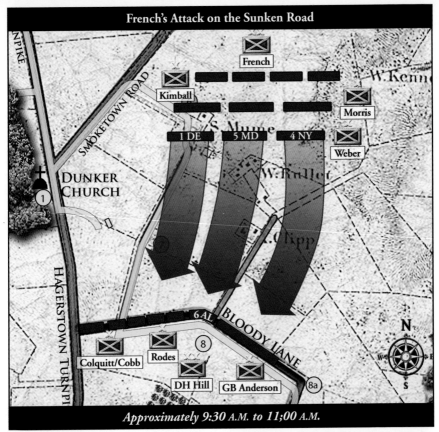

French's Attack on the Sunken Road

French

Kimball

Morris

1 DE   5 MD   4 NY

Weber

DUNKER CHURCH

W. Kenn

W. Roulette

N. Clipp

6 AL   BLOODY LANE

Colquitt/Cobb   Rodes   8

DH Hill   GB Anderson   8a

Approximately 9:30 A.M. to 11;00 A.M.

Brigadier General William H. French was known as "Old Blinky" for his habit of blinking his eyes while he talked. A West Point graduate of 1837, French served in the Mexican War and was later given command of Fort Meade, an outpost in the Florida interior. While there, he and one of his subordinates, Thomas Jackson, became embroiled in a feud. Jackson accused French of impropriety with a servant girl, an accusation that led to Jackson's arrest and prompted the future Confederate hero to resign from the army to pursue a teaching position at the Virginia Military Institute (VMI). French was transferred and ended up commanding a garrison in Texas. When the Civil War broke out, French refused to surrender the garrison. Instead he marched his troops to the Gulf of Mexico and sailed to a Federal outpost in Key West, Florida.

Brig. General William H. French

John B. Gordon

1832-1904

Born in Upson City, Georgia, Gordon was a lawyer turned soldier. After recruiting a volunteer company of infantry called the "Raccoon Roughs," from the states of Alabama, Georgia and Tennessee, his men were assigned to the 6th Alabama in 1861. Gordon proved himself an able leader and rose to command a Corps by the end of the war. At Antietam, Gordon promised General Lee that his men would stay in their positions in the Sunken Road "until the sun went down or victory was won." He did his best to live up to his word. He was shot five times before falling unconscious into a pool of blood. The fifth and final bullet pierced his left cheek and exited his jaw. Gordon recovered from his wounds, but thereafter often posed in profile to hide the disfiguring scar. Following the war, Gordon went into politics, serving three terms as a U.S. Senator from Georgia and then a term as the state's governor.

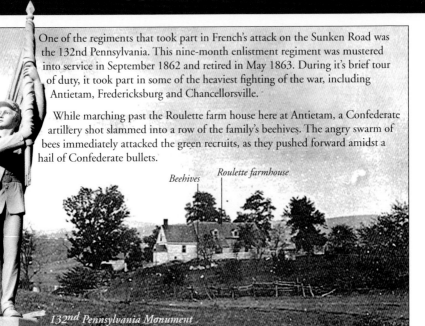

One of the regiments that took part in French's attack on the Sunken Road was the 132nd Pennsylvania. This nine-month enlistment regiment was mustered into service in September 1862 and retired in May 1863. During it's brief tour of duty, it took part in some of the heaviest fighting of the war, including Antietam, Fredericksburg and Chancellorsville.

While marching past the Roulette farm house here at Antietam, a Confederate artillery shot slammed into a row of the family's beehives. The angry swarm of bees immediately attacked the green recruits, as they pushed forward amidst a hail of Confederate bullets.

Beehives

Roulette farmhouse

132nd Pennsylvania Monument

Bloody Lane

132nd PA Monument

Dunker Church

Visitor Center

New York State Monument

1 DE

Weber

5 MD

4 NY

6?

2 NC

14 NC

4 NC

30 NC

Brigadier General Max Weber's three regiments, the 1st Delaware, 5th Maryland and 4th New York, were the first to run into the Confederates in the Sunken Road.

Col. Charles Courtenay Tew

Colonel Charles Courtenay Tew had just assumed command of Anderson's brigade when a bullet struck him in the left temple. Barely alive, he was approached in the Bloody Lane by an Ohio soldier who attempted to take the sword lying across the colonel's knees. Suddenly, Tew "drew it toward his body with the last of his remaining strength, and then his grasp relaxed and he fell forward, dead." Because Tew's body was never recovered, conflicting accounts of his fate circulated back home to his anguished family for years. In 1873 the matter was finally put to rest when a former Federal officer, Captain J.W. Bean, confirmed that he had buried Tew shortly after the battle. He also returned a silver cup, right, inscribed with the colonel's initials. It's believed that the body lying against the side of the Sunken Road in the lower right corner of the photograph below is that of Colonel Tew.

Mathew Brady

Circa 1823 - 1896

The Civil War was the first conflict in history to be extensively documented with photography. Much of the credit for that goes to Mathew Brady. Spotting an opportunity to capture history and make a profit, Brady employed a cadre of photographers to venture onto the battlefields and document the great spectacle of war. Brady spent over $100,000 to amass a collection of nearly six thousand images. Unfortunately, the gamble never paid off. Bankrupt, he eventually sold his collection to the government for a paltry $25,000. His Antietam series, photographed by Alexander Gardner and James Gibson, remain to this day some of the most striking images of war ever photographed.

Civil War Photography

Invented in 1839, photography was still in its pioneering stages when America went to war with itself in 1861. The earliest form of photography, daguerreotype, produced an image on a chemically treated silver plate. It was a complex process that did not lend itself to mass production. By 1861, however, two new technologies had set the stage for photographers to bring the war home for public consumption like never before. First, glass plate negatives, invented in 1851, allowed photographers the ability to mass produce their images onto paper, making them affordable and widely available. Second, stereoscopic photographs exploded onto the scene in the late 1850s. The 3-D photo craze made it profitable for photographers to document and print a wide variety of subjects. It is estimated that some 70 percent of the photographs taken during the war were stereoscopic. Many famous images that you see in this book and other Civil War publications are in fact just one of two original stereo pictures.

The photographer would remove the lens cover and expose a light-sensitive plate inside the camera for 3-20 seconds, depending on the light conditions.

Stereoscopic Camera

Two lenses that approximate the spacing of human eyes record slightly different perspectives of the same scene.

A pair of images was recorded onto a single light-sensitive glass negative.

Stereoscopic prints were made from the glass negative.

Studio Camera

A dark cloth was used to keep light out, while the photographer focused the image in the back of the camera.

Stereograph Viewer

A special viewer allowed each eye to see only one of the pair of images, forcing the brain to merge the two and create the 3-D illusion.

Wagons were used as portable darkrooms. Photographers had to coat a glass plate with chemicals; transfer it in a light-proof box to the camera; expose it; and return it to the wagon to develop, before the chemical coating dried. This was called the "wet plate" process.

1823-1867

Irish revolutionist, exiled convict, escapee, Civil War general and Montana governor, Thomas Francis Meagher (pronounced mär) lived an interesting life. Condemned to death for his part in the failed Irish Rebellion of 1848, his sentence was commuted to exile on the island of Tasmania.

Meagher was responsible for introducing the tricolor flag that became Ireland's National Flag.

By 1852, Meagher had escaped and found his way to New York City, where in 1861-62, he recruited the Irish Brigade. Meagher led the brigade through some of the hardest fighting of the war, including the Bloody Lane at Antietam and the Stone Wall at Fredericksburg. In 1867 Meagher was serving as acting governor of Montana when he mysteriously fell off a steamboat into the Missouri River and is presumed to have drowned. His body was never found.

Irish Brigade Monument

Meagher

Meagher

| | | | | |
| 29 MA | 63 NY | 69 NY | 88 NY |

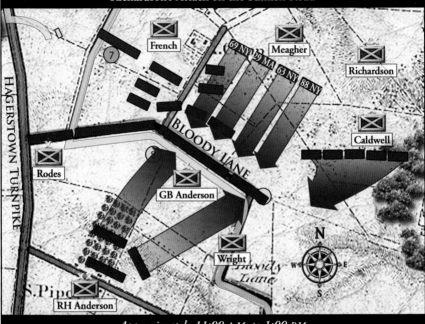

Richardson's Attack on the Sunken Road

Approximately 11:00 A.M. to 1:00 P.M.

Maj. Gen. Israel Richardson

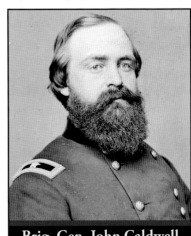

Brig. Gen. John Caldwell

James Longstreet

James Longstreet, General Lee's "old war horse," served the Confederate army from Bull Run all the way to its surrender at Appomattox. His attacks at Second Manassas and Chickamauga produced two of the South's greatest victories, while his attack at Gettysburg on day three (Pickett's Charge) produced one of its worst defeats. Following the war, Longstreet's decision to join the Republican party alienated him from many of his former comrades. Related to Ulyses S. Grant by marriage, he accepted a position in President Grant's administration and went on to serve as Ambassador to Turkey. In 1897, eight years after his wife Louise died, he remarried at the age of 76 to the 34-year-old Helen Dortch.

Double Canister by Dale Gallon

Major General James Longstreet directing fire in the Piper orchard

Brigadier General George B. Anderson was a West Point graduate from the class of 1852. On the afternoon of September 17, his four North Carolina regiments defended the eastern portion of the Sunken Road. While extolling his men to fight, Anderson was wounded in the foot and forced to relinquish command. He was eventually transported to Raleigh North Carolina to recover from what was supposed to be a minor wound. Unfortunately, his foot became infected and turned septic. Despite the amputation of his leg, Anderson died on October 16, 1862, just one day prior to his daughter's birth.

G.B. Anderson

41

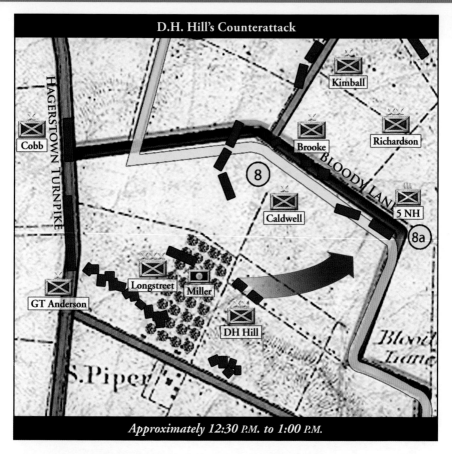

D.H. Hill's Counterattack

Approximately 12:30 P.M. to 1:00 P.M.

Maj. Gen. D. H. Hill

Major General Daniel Harvey Hill, like his brother-in-law, Stonewall Jackson, was devoutly religious and believed that his fate lay in God's hands. If Hill was correct in his beliefs, then God was looking out for him at Antietam. During the course of the battle, Hill was conferring with Lee and Longstreet and refused to make himself less conspicuous by dismounting from his horse. A Federal battery spotted him and opened fire. Longstreet saw the puff of smoke and said, "there is a shot for you." According to Longstreet, the gun was a mile away and the cannon shot came whisking through the air for three or four seconds before it took off the front legs of the horse that Hill sat on, letting the animal down upon its stumps and leaving Hill unscathed. Hill would survive the war, but eventually succumb to stomach cancer in 1889 at the age of sixty.

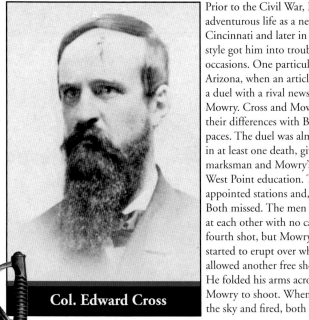

Col. Edward Cross

Prior to the Civil War, Edward Cross led an adventurous life as a newspaperman and editor in Cincinnati and later in Arizona. His incendiary style got him into trouble on a number of occasions. One particular close call happened in Arizona, when an article Cross published led to a duel with a rival newspaper editor, Sylvester Mowry. Cross and Mowry vowed to resolve their differences with Burnside Carbines at forty paces. The duel was almost guaranteed to result in at least one death, given Cross' reputation as a marksman and Mowry's former army career and West Point education. The two men stood in their appointed stations and, on cue, turned and fired. Both missed. The men fired two more rounds at each other with no casualties. Cross got off a fourth shot, but Mowry's gun misfired. As a fight started to erupt over whether Mowry should be allowed another free shot, Cross settled the matter. He folded his arms across his chest and told Mowry to shoot. When Mowry pointed his gun to the sky and fired, both men declared the duel over.

Revolver

Colonel Cross's Sword and Revolver
(Courtesy of the Lancaster New Hampshire Historical Society)

The Observation Tower
Build in 1896 by the War Department, the tower was and still is used to train military personnel in this outdoor battlefield classroom. The War Department was the original administrator of the park, when it was established in 1890. The National Park Service took control in 1933.

Sword

Irish Brigade Monument

Richardson's Memorial Cannon

Observation Tower

Ambrose E. Burnside

1824 -1881

The man who made cheek hair fashionable also invented a breech loading rifle that bears his name, the Burnside Carbine. After his rifle company went bankrupt, an old friend from West Point, George McClellan, stepped in and offered Burnside a job at the Illinois Central Railroad. Their friendship soured at Antietam, however. Following the battle, Lincoln replaced McClellan with Burnside to lead the Army of the Potomac. He commanded it for a single battle, Fredericksburg, and suffered one of the worst defeats of the war.

Burnside Carbine

Robert Toombs

Alfred Waud's sketch depicting Union troops taking the bridge.

Following the war, Toombs was known as the "Unreconstructed Rebel." He never swore an oath of allegiance to the United States government.

a nat'l "chokepoint"

Burnside Bridge was called Rohrbach or Lower Bridge prior to the battle

This historic tree still grows next to the bridge

Toombs' men occupied the steep hillside overlooking the bridge

Union troops huddled behind this stone wall for protection

Brig. Gen. Edward Ferrero

Prior to the Civil War, Edward Ferrero was a successful dance instructor. In 1859 he published *The Art of Dancing*, a popular manual with instructions on all the latest dances, such as the Polka and the Five Step Waltz. When the war broke out, Ferrero turned in his dance shoes and raised the 51st New York Regiment, known as the "Shepard Rifles." By Antietam, Ferrero led a brigade. During his assault on the bridge, the men of his former regiment sustained 87 casualties, including one officer and eighteen men killed. Ferrero went on to lead a division of colored troops in the IX Corps. His men suffered grievous casualties during a valiant effort to breach the Crater at Petersburg on July 30, 1864.

51st Pennsylvania Infantry Monument

This photograph, taken by Alexander Gardner on September 21, 1862, shows a soldier standing behind the graves of twelve men from the 51st New York, Ferrero's former regiment. The men were killed while taking Burnside Bridge, which is partially visible in the background.

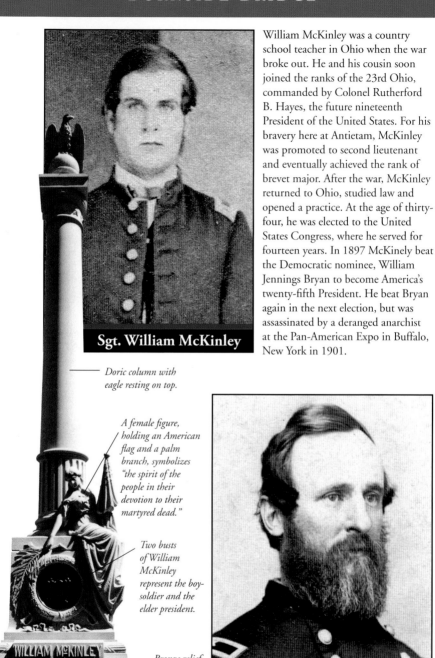

William McKinley was a country school teacher in Ohio when the war broke out. He and his cousin soon joined the ranks of the 23rd Ohio, commanded by Colonel Rutherford B. Hayes, the future nineteenth President of the United States. For his bravery here at Antietam, McKinley was promoted to second lieutenant and eventually achieved the rank of brevet major. After the war, McKinley returned to Ohio, studied law and opened a practice. At the age of thirty-four, he was elected to the United States Congress, where he served for fourteen years. In 1897 McKinely beat the Democratic nominee, William Jennings Bryan to become America's twenty-fifth President. He beat Bryan again in the next election, but was assassinated by a deranged anarchist at the Pan-American Expo in Buffalo, New York in 1901.

Sgt. William McKinley

Doric column with eagle resting on top.

A female figure, holding an American flag and a palm branch, symbolizes "the spirit of the people in their devotion to their martyred dead."

Two busts of William McKinley represent the boy-soldier and the elder president.

WILLIAM McKINLEY

Bronze relief of McKinley serving his comrades under fire.

Col. Rutherford B. Hayes

JANUARY 29, 1843 — SEPTEMBER 14, 1901

William McKinley Monument

American Zouaves

American Zouave fighting units, Union and Confederate, were modeled after the elite Zouave French light infantry of North Africa, whose brightly colored garb and fighting spirit were the stuff of legend. Elmer Ellsworth, a personal friend of Abraham Lincoln, is the man credited with bringing the Zouave traditions to America. In the years prior to the Civil War, Ellsworth toured the United States with his elite drill team and dazzled audiences with their colorful garb and precise movements. Shortly after the outbreak of the war, Ellsworth found himself marching

DEATH OF COL. ELLSWORTH.

with a force sent to seize Alexandria Virginia. Noticing a Confederate flag flying atop the Marshall House hotel, he ascended and tore it down. At the bottom of the stairs, Ellsworth was greeted by the innkeeper, who had sworn to kill the man who tried to take down his flag. A shotgun blast killed Ellsworth instantly. President Lincoln was overcome by the loss of his friend and ordered Ellsworth's body to lie in state in the East Room of the White House. "Avenge Ellsworth" became the rallying cry that led to the formation of quite a few Zouave regiments. Even before Ellsworth's death, Colonel Rush Hawkins had organized the 9th New York, the first Zouave regiment mustered into service. The regiment's motto was "Toujours Pret," meaning "Always Ready."

Rush Hawkins

Uniform & Equipment of the 9th New York Zouaves

— Fez

— Blue tassel

— Blanket roll

— Knapsack

— Canteen

— Brass belt plate

— Cartridge box

— Bayonet

1853 Enfield Rifle

— Short jacket

— Red sash

— Cap box

Wool pantaloons

— Leggings

Burnside's Attack

SHARPSBURG

Garnett

Jenkins

Evans

Drayton

DR Jones

Kemper

Willcox

BURNSIDE BRIDGE

Sturgis

Fairchild

Toombs

Harland

Rodman

ANTIETAM CREEK

Approximately 3:15 P.M.

General Isaac Rodman was a Quaker from Rhode Island whose middle name was Peace. He was serving in the state senate when the war broke out. Choosing devotion to his country over the pacifist roots of his religion, Rodman organized a company of infantry and joined the 2nd Rhode Island. Rising through the ranks, he led a division at Antietam.

Brig. General Isaac P. Rodman

Monument to Hawkins' Zouaves, 9th New York Infantry Regiment

Always Ready The 9th New York Hawkins' Zouaves at Antietam by Keith Rocco

Robert E. Lee

1807 - 1870

Born January 19, 1807, in Westmoreland County, Virginia, Robert E. Lee was the son of an American Revolutionary War hero and related by marriage to George Washington. Lee was, however, first and foremost a Virginian, a descendant of one of the "First Families" of the Old Dominion.

In 1829, Lee graduated second in his West Point class without a single demerit and was commissioned a brevet second lieutenant of Engineers. During the war with Mexico, Lee performed scouting missions and was promoted to colonel for distinguished conduct. He went on to become Superintendent of West Point for a time and in 1859 led a contingent of Marines to capture John Brown at Harper's Ferry.

Shortly before Virginia withdrew from the Union, President Lincoln offered Lee command of Union forces to put down the rebellion. Lee could not bring himself to raise his sword against his native state and instead cast his lot with the Confederacy. All three of his sons also served in the Confederate army. His youngest, Robert E. Lee Jr. was a private in the Rockbridge Artillery at Antietam.

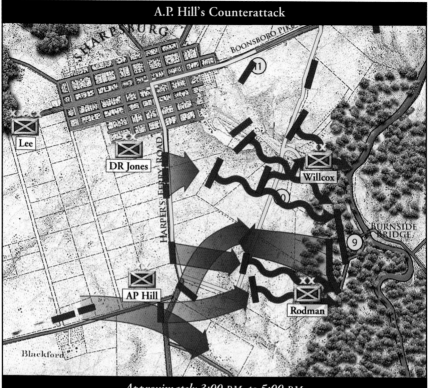

A.P. Hill's Counterattack

Approximately 3:00 P.M. to 5:00 P.M.

Lt. John A. Ramsay

Maj. Gen. A.P. Hill

Lieutenant Ramsay's Telescope

George B. McClellan

1826 - 1885

George Brinton McClellan was born December 3, 1826 to a prominent Philadelphia family. He excelled at school, entering West Point at only 15 years of age. Like Lee, he graduated second in his class and was appointed second lieutenant in the Corps of Engineers. He served with gallantry in the war with Mexico and was breveted twice.

He spent three years teaching at West Point and was sent overseas to observe European methods of warfare during the Crimean War. His experience in Europe inspired him to develop a new type of horse saddle. The "McClellan saddle" became standard issue for the cavalry until 1942, when the army replaced horses with mechanized equipment.

Known as "Little Mac" or "Young Napoleon," McClellan was a first rate organizer, but a timid field commander. Following the Battle of Antietam, McClellan refused to pursue Lee's army until he was satisfied that his men were thoroughly resupplied and recuperated. Lincoln finally lost his patience and replaced McClellan with General Burnside on November 7, 1862. McClellan never held another position in the Union army. In the 1864 Presidential election he ran as a Democrat against Lincoln and lost. He went on to serve as governor of New Jersey from 1878-1881.

Drag using bayonet drawn into hook

60% of Confederates dead - unknown

Five days after the Battle of Antietam, President Lincoln issued the preliminary Emancipation Proclamation. It stated that on January 1, 1863, all slaves in any State then in rebellion "...shall be then, thenceforward, and forever free." Human liberty was now a central purpose of America's struggle to save the Union. If the losses suffered by Lee at Antietam were not enough to dissuade European powers from aiding the Confederacy, then Lincoln's new cause would be.

President Lincoln reading the Emancipation Proclamation to his cabinet.

4700 Union Soldiers

Attempting to prod McClellan into pursuing Lee's retreating army, President Lincoln paid a surprise visit to the Antietam battlefield on October 1. Looking at an expanse of white tents, Lincoln remarked that this was not the Army of the Potomac, but rather "McClellan's bodyguard."

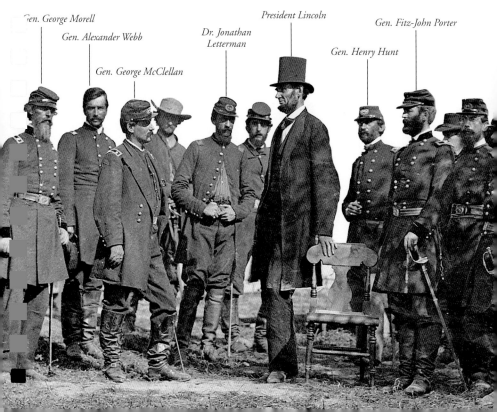

Gen. George Morell

Gen. Alexander Webb

Gen. George McClellan

Dr. Jonathan Letterman

President Lincoln

Gen. Henry Hunt

Gen. Fitz-John Porter

Did you know?

The identities of approximately forty-two percent of soldiers who died on the battlefields of the Civil War are known only to God. The Civil War, in fact, provided the first documented attempts by soldiers to ensure that their identities would be known, in the event they were killed during battle. Solutions to this problem were varied. At the battle of Mine's Run in 1863, for example, Union General Meade's troops pinned their names to their uniforms. Other soldiers made or purchased identification tags made of a variety of materials.

Personal Identification Tag

Union burial crew on the Miller farm

More than 620,000 Americans perished during the Civil War, making it the deadliest conflict in the history of the United States. This graph depicts the number of American deaths by conflict. Source: U.S. Army Military History Institute, Carlisle, PA.

Conflict	American Deaths
American Revolution	4,435
War of 1812	2,260
Mexican War	13,283
Civil War	623,026
Spanish American War	2,446
World War I	116,708
World War II	407,316
Korean Conflict	36,914
Vietnam Conflict	58,169
Gulf War	269
Iraq War	4,847

Did you know?

Antietam National Cemetery was closed for new burials in 1953. However, an exception was made for Navy Seaman Patrick Howard Roy who in 2000 was killed in the terrorist attack on the USS Cole, while it was docked in Yemen. Roy, a Maryland native, grew up in the small town of Keedysville, about three miles from the Antietam battlefield.

Antietam National Cemetery

NOT FOR THEMSELVES BUT FOR THEIR COUNTRY

SEPTEMBER 17, 1862

U.S. Soldier Monument

CREDITS

TravelBrains sincerely thanks the following individuals and organizations for their contributions to the development of the Antietam Expedition Guide.

Individuals

Ted Alexander
Jackie Barton
James Blake
Tom Clemens
Brian Downey
Myra Emerson
John Fieseler

Dennis Frye
Anne Gallon
Dale Gallon
Jeff Giambrone
Rob Gibson
Stephanie Gray

Lance Herdegen
John Howard
Faith Kent
Mike Pride
John E. Ramsay, Jr.
Keith Rocco

Terry Reimer
Edward D. Sloan, Jr.
Brent Smith
Keith Snyder
David Vermilion
Gigi Yelton
Bob Zeller

Organizations

Antietam on the Web www.aotw.org
Center for Civil War Photography
   www.civilwarphotography.org
Gallon Historical Art, Gettysburg, PA
   www.gallon.com
Gibson's Photographic Gallery
Hagerstown-Washington County CVB
Library of Congress
Maryland office of Tourism

National Archives and Records Administration
National Museum of Civil War Medicine
Old Court House Museum, Vicksburg, Mississippi
State Historical Society of Wisconsin
Tourism Council of Frederick County
Tradition Studios, Woodstock, VA
   www.keithrocco.com
United States Army Military History Institute,
Carlisle Barracks, PA

Music

Brent Smith
Lennon Leppert

Zouave Reenactor ....Shaun Grenan

Voice Actors

Audio Tour Narrator ....Reg Green
Audio Tour Guide ....Debby Winsberg
Union Voices................................Terence Rae
Confederate Voices ....Lance Smith

TravelBrains Antietam Team

Catherine Davis
Paul Davis
Victor Davis

Book Image Credits

Expedition Guide Cover: "Always Ready" by 7: Library of Congress, MASS-MOLLUS/USAMHI, Carlisle, PA. 9: Library of Congress. 11. MASS-MOLLUS/USAMHI, Library of Congress. 17: MASS-MOLLUS/ USAMHI. National Museum of Civil War Medicine. 19 Library of Congress. 20: Library of Congress. 21:National Archives. 22: MASS-MOLLUS/USAMHI, National Archives. 23: The Dawes Arboretum, "Through the Cornfield" by Keith Rocco, Tradition Studios www.keithrocco.com. 24 25: The Iron Brigade courtesy the Wisconsin Historical Society, MASS-MOLLUS/USAMHI, Dirty Billy's Hats www. dirtybillyshats.com, Texas State Library and Archives Commission 26: MASS-MOLLUS/USAMHI. 27: Deeds of Valor, The Institute for Civil War Studies, Carroll College, Waukesha, Wisconsin. 28-29: Library of Congress. 30: MASS-MOLLUS/USAMHI. 32: MASS-MOLLUS/USAMHI. 33: Library of Congress 34: National Park Service. 35: Edward D. Sloan, Jr., Library of Congress. 36: Library of Congress. 37: Studio stereoscopic cameras courtesy Gibson's Photographic Gallery, stereographic viewer courtesy Bob Zeller, Library of Congress. 38: MASS-MOLLUS/USAMHI. 39: MASS MOLLUS/USAMHI. 40-41: "Double Canister" by Dale Gallon, image courtesy of Gallon Historical Art, Gettysburg, PA www.gallon. com, MASS-MOLLUS/USAMHI. 42: MASS-MOLLUS/USAMHI. 43: MASS-MOLLUS/USAMHI, Cross's artifacts courtesy of Lancaster Historical Society. 44: Library of Congress. 45: MASS-MOLLUS/ USAMHI, Library of Congress. 46: MASS-MOLLUS/USAMHI, Library of Congress. 47: Rutherford B. Hayes Presidential Center. 48: Library of Congress. 49: MASS-MOLLUS/USAMHI. 50-51: "Always Ready" by Keith Rocco, Tradition Studios www.keithrocco.com. 52: Library of Congress. 53: Image of Lt. John Ramsay and telescope courtesy of John E. Ramsay, Jr., image of A.P. Hill courtesy of the Old Court House Museum, Vicksburg, Mississippi. 54: Library of Congress. 55: Library of Congress.56-57: Library of Congress, dog tags courtesy of Courtesy of Motts Military Museum, Groveport, OH.

HELP PRESERVE YOUR ANTIETAM

Preserving the hallowed ground at Sharpsburg Maryland is a tribute to our nation and a fitting way to honor those who fought here on September 17, 1862. The text on the Private Soldier Monument in Antietam National Cemetery –"Not for themselves but for their country"— underscores the events of that day and why Antietam National Battlefield should be forever protected.

Private funding is increasingly critical for land acquisition, battlefield restoration and visitor services. The ANTIETAM PARTNER program supports these initiatives by raising funds and partnering with individuals and organizations that share our commitment to preserving this special place. Join with us today by becoming an ANTIETAM PARTNER. For details visit us on the web at AntietamMuseumStore.com or call 301/432-4329. Proceeds from this Expedition Guide support Antietam National Battlefield.

ANTIETAM PARTNER™ is a program of the Western Maryland Interpretive Association (WMIA). WMIA, PO Box 692, Sharpsburg, MD 21782

CONTRIBUTING ARTISTS

TravelBrains is proud to feature the artwork of two renowned Civil War artists, Dale Gallon and Keith Rocco, in our Antietam guidebook. To learn more about these artists and view their artwork, visit them online at the websites listed below.

DALE GALLON
Gallon Historical Art, Inc.
9 Steinwehr Ave.
Gettysburg, PA 17325
(717) 334-0430
info@gallon.com
www.gallon.com

KEITH ROCCO
TRADITION STUDIOS
Woodstock, Virginia 22664
(540) 459-5469
krocco@shentel.net
www.keithrocco.com

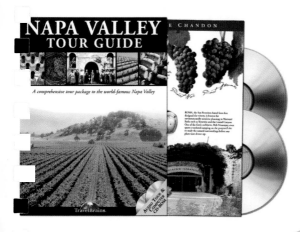

Yellowstone Expedition Guide

www.TravelBrains.com

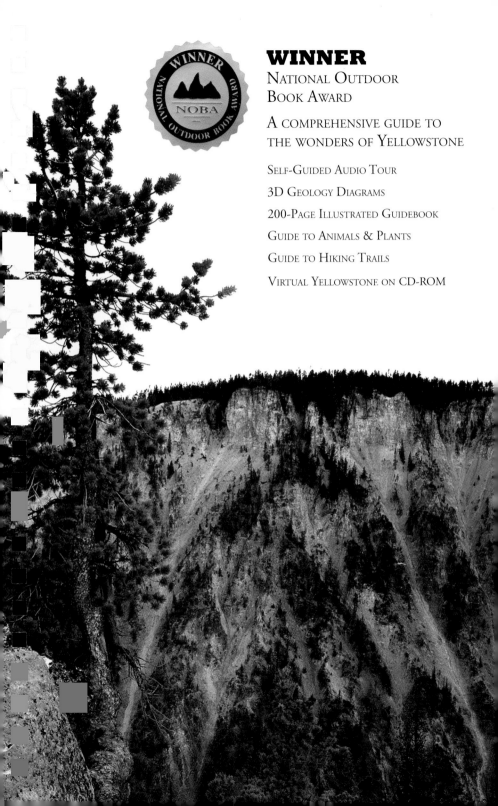

WINNER
NATIONAL OUTDOOR
BOOK AWARD

A COMPREHENSIVE GUIDE TO
THE WONDERS OF YELLOWSTONE

SELF-GUIDED AUDIO TOUR

3D GEOLOGY DIAGRAMS

200-PAGE ILLUSTRATED GUIDEBOOK

GUIDE TO ANIMALS & PLANTS

GUIDE TO HIKING TRAILS

VIRTUAL YELLOWSTONE ON CD-ROM

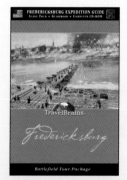

MARYLAND CAMPAIGN TRAIL

The Antietam Campaign Trail

A guide to the historic sites along Maryland's Civil War Trails

Official Trails Sign

This guide will take you to some of the key historic sites along Maryland's Civil War Trails associated with the Antietam Campaign. As you drive, keep an eye out for the signs marked with red bugles. These Maryland Civil War Trails markers will take you to wayside exhibits that explain the history of the Civil War in Maryland. For a complete listing of all the sites along the trail, pick up or order a copy of the official guide to Maryland's Civil War Trails, available at visitor centers or by calling toll free (888) 248-4597. You can also find information online at www.civilwartrails.org. The Antietam Campaign trail can be completed in one day, but take your time and stay an extra day or two if you can.

Official Trails Guide

THE CAMPAIGN BEGINS

White's Ford
(C&O Canal NHP)

On September 4, 1862, as a Confederate band played "Maryland, My Maryland," Lee's army splashed across a waist-deep section of the Potomac River at White's Ford near the town of Leesburg, Virginia. The campaign had begun.

Union scouts take aim at Lee's army crossing the Potomac

Side Trips

 Loudoun Museum in Leesburg, VA: Leesburg was the staging point for the Maryland invasion.

White's Ferry: take the General Jubal Early ferry across the Potomac River.

Monocacy Aqueduct: site of a failed Confederate attempt to destroy it.

Poolesville: site of cavalry skirmishes on September 5 & 8, 1862.

In 1862, the Potomac River was, for all intents and purposes, a hostile international border, separating the Confederacy from the Union. Lee crossed the border, hoping that the presence of his army might persuade sympathizers in the border state of Maryland to throw off the "yoke of Union oppression" and join the Confederate cause. Unfortunately for Lee, he found little sympathy for the South in this rural section of the state.

1

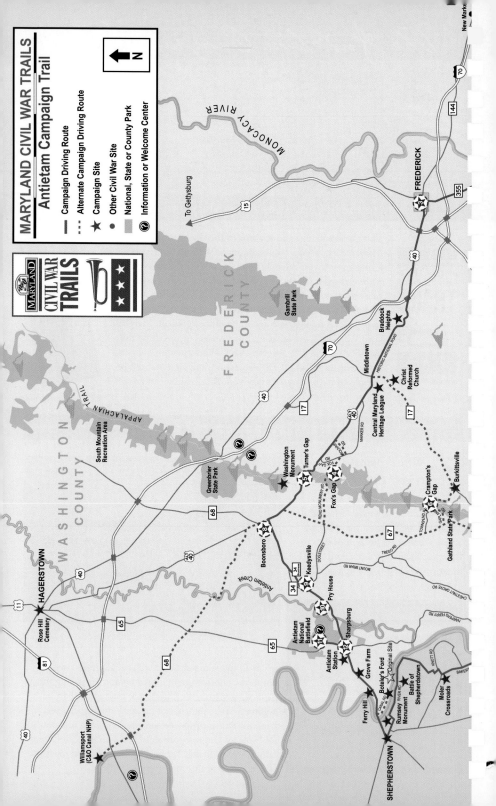

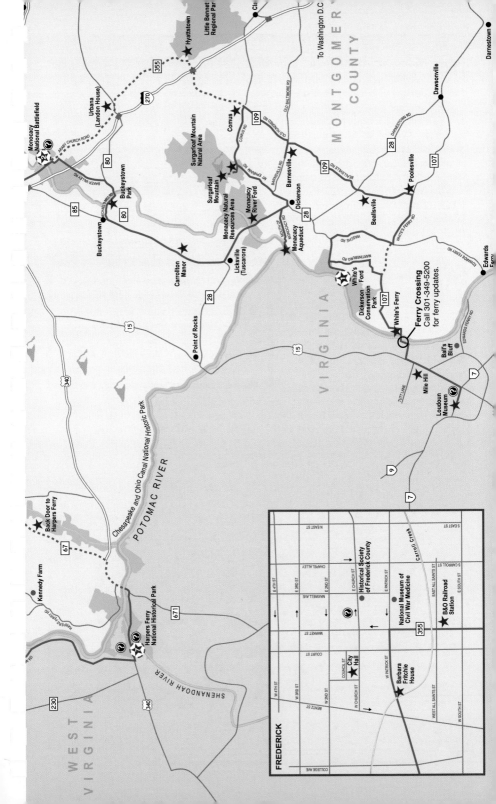

② Monocacy Battlefield

A copy of Lee's Special Orders 191 was discovered in an abandoned Confederate campsite on land that is now part of the Monocacy National Battlefield. A soldier in the 27th Indiana discovered Lee's lost orders wrapped around several cigars somewhere in the vicinity of the Best Farm. The battlefield is also the site of Confederate General Jubal A. Early's failed attempt to attack Washington D.C. that culminated in the Battle of Monocacy in July 1864.

Special Orders 191

③ Frederick

When General McClellan arrived in Frederick on September 13, 1862, he received a warm welcome from the local residents. "The whole population turned out, wild with joy," wrote a Federal officer. "When McClellan appeared, the crowd became so demonstrative that we were forcibly brought to a halt." That same day,

Frederick Points of Interest

★ **National Museum of Civil War Medicine :** tells the medical story of the Civil War.

★ **Barbara Fritchie House:** Whittier's famous ballad about the old lady who shamed Stonewall Jackson.

★ **Historic District Walking Tours:** Stop by or call the visitor center for details.

McClellan would come into possession of Lee's operation plans (Special Orders 191). "Here is a paper with which if I cannot beat Bobby Lee, I will be willing to go home!" exclaimed McClellan. The discovery of Lee's plans set the stage for the Battle of South Mountain.

General McClellan riding through Frederick on his horse, Dan Webster

Lee

Boonsboro

Longstreet

DH Hill

Turner's Gap

Hooker

Fox's Gap

Bolivar

Reno

McClellan

National Road

Old Sharpsburg Road

South Mountain

N

W — E

S

Crampton Gap

McLaws

Franklin

Burkittsville

Scale in Miles

0   1   2   3

5

Fox's Gap & Turner's Gap

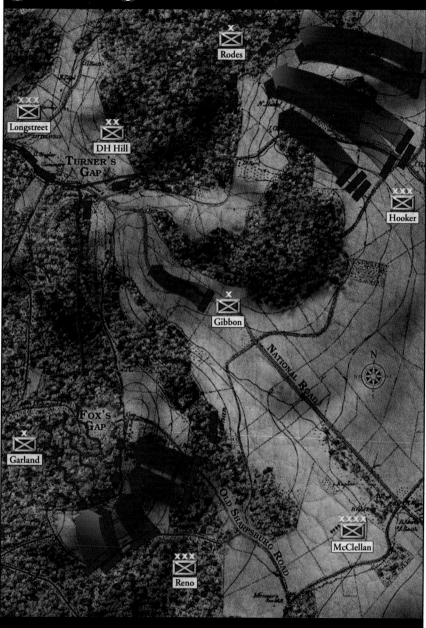

On the morning of September 14th, from his lookout atop Turner's Gap, Confederate General D.H. Hill observed what he called, "the vast army of McClellan spread out before him." His lone division of some 5,000 men would have to hold back the sea of Federals until General Longstreet's reinforcements could arrive.

Joseph Hooker

Rutherford B. Hayes

Jesse Reno

James Longstreet

Samuel Garland

THE BATTLE STARTED around 9 a.m. at Fox's Gap, about a mile south of Turner's Gap. A thinly stretched Confederate brigade under the command of General Samuel Garland defended the area. Outnumbered three to one, the North Carolinians put up a dogged resistance, but were forced to retreat. Garland was mortally wounded in the fighting and future U.S. President, Rutherford B. Hayes, commanding the 23rd Ohio, was wounded. The dramatized sketch below depicts both events.

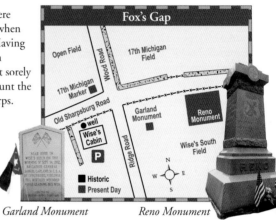

By the afternoon, the Confederates were on the brink of collapse at Fox's Gap when Longstreet's reinforcements arrived. Having completed a thirteen mile march from Hagerstown, his troops were tired, but sorely needed. Their timely arrival helped blunt the renewed assaults by the Union IX Corps.

When the IX Corps commander, General Jesse Reno, rode forward to assess the situation, he was shot and mortally wounded - not far from the spot where Confederate General Garland had been mortally wounded. Today, both commanders have monuments dedicated to them at Fox's Gap.

Garland Monument

Reno Monument

Rutherford B. Hayes

Samuel Garland

AT TURNER'S GAP, Union General Joseph Hooker's I Corps began advancing up the steep slopes of South Mountain sometime after 4 p.m. The bulk of his force swung north of Turner's Gap in a flanking maneuver, while a single brigade was assigned the arduous task of marching directly up the National Road in a direct assault on the gap. The lone brigade, composed of Midwesterners from Wisconsin and Indiana, was commanded by Brigadier General John Gibbon.

From his headquarters, Union General George McClellan watched through his telescope as Gibbon's men battled against great odds along the pike leading up to the gap. Legend has it that McClellan turned to General Hooker and remarked, "They must be made of iron." "By the eternal, they are of iron," was Hooker's reply and from that day forward, Gibbon's men were known as the "Iron Brigade."

While Gibbon's men were fighting, the bulk of the I Corps made it onto the ridge north of Turner's Gap and turned south towards the pass. Darkness brought an end to the fighting, but the Confederate defense was no longer tenable. On the evening of September 14, 1862, General Lee ordered his troops to withdraw to Boonsboro, while the Confederate commander contemplated ending the campaign and returning to Virginia. The next day, however, Lee would receive a piece of news from Stonewall Jackson at Harpers Ferry that would change his mind and convince him to stay and fight in Maryland.

Brigadier General John Gibbon

Turner's Gap Point of Interest

★ **Washington Monument State Park:** Erected in 1827, the Washington Monument on South Mountain was the first one in the United States constructed in honor of George Washington. During the Antietam Campaign, the Federals used the monument as a signal station. The view from the top is spectacular.

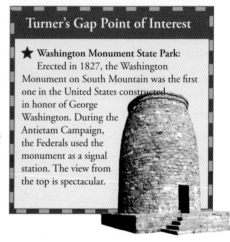

Farmer Daniel Wise's property witnessed much of the action at Fox's Gap. Following the battle, his well became the final resting place for many Confederate dead.

Wise farmhouse

Old Sharpsburg Road

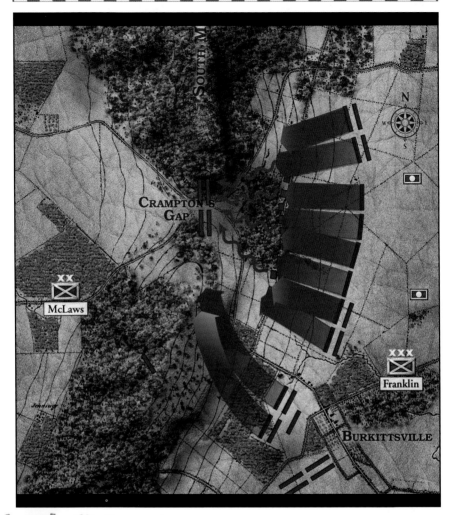

Crampton's Gap

Union General William Franklin's VI Corps, 12,000 men strong, had the vital mission of breaking the siege at Harpers Ferry. Standing in their way at Crampton's Gap were 1,000 Confederates, commanded by Colonel Thomas Munford. Franklin overestimated the force in front of him and spent much of the day making attack preparations. Shortly after 3 p.m. the Federals launched their attack on a front more than a mile wide. By dusk, they had driven the Confederates off the mountain, but Franklin chose not to pursue them into Pleasant Valley. Had he done so, he might have interrupted or perhaps ended the siege of Harpers Ferry. Years later, in 1896, Civil War journalist George Alfred Townsend constructed a giant arch at Crampton's Gap to commemorate Civil War correspondents and artists.

War Correspondents Arch

9

HARPERS FERRY OCCUPIED A STRATEGIC LOCATION at the confluence of the Potomac and Shenandoah Rivers. The high bluffs and hills that surrounded the town made it vulnerable to attack. Lee took advantage of the weakness, sending three separate commands to surround the garrison.

Col. Dixon Miles

Stonewall Jackson marched the largest of the three forces 51 miles in four days to approach Harpers Ferry from the west. Brigadier General John Walker took his 4,000 man division south and captured Loudoun Heights, overlooking Harpers Ferry on the Virginia side of the Potomac. General Lafayette McLaws was ordered to take Maryland Heights to the east of the town. After a brief fight on the western slope of Maryland Heights on September 13, McLaws captured the strategic precipice and dragged four cannons to the summit. By September 14, Confederate gun crews were pounding the Federal garrison with impunity from Luodoun and Maryland Heights. Meanwhile, Jackson was positioning his large force for a decisive attack on Boulivar Heights.

The task of defending Harpers Ferry fell on the shoulders of Colonel Dixon Miles. A veteran of 38 years in the old army, Miles had been stationed at Harpers Ferry after a military court of inquiry determined that he had been drunk while commanding his troops at the Battle of Bull Run. By September 14, Miles was hemmed in on all sides and unable to return fire at the Confederate guns shelling his troops from the heights. The next day he surrendered the garrison: 12,500 men, 73 artillery pieces, and over 11,000 small arms. It was the largest surrender of U.S. troops in history and remained so until the fall of the Philippines in World War II. The only significant portion of the garrison that escaped capture was 1,500 cavalry troops that had crossed the Potomac River on a pontoon bridge under the cover of darkness the night before.

7 Harpers Ferry

Maj. Gen. Thomas "Stonewall" Jackson

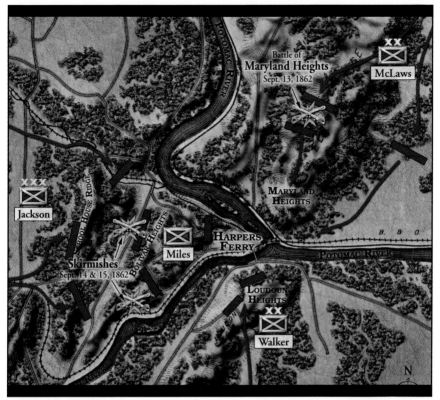

Jackson did not have much time to savor the victory at Harpers Ferry. Lee needed his troops urgently in Sharpsburg, Maryland. Jackson responded to Lee's call, marching the bulk of his troops through the night, arriving in Sharpsburg on the 16th of September. The following morning, Jackson's troops endured the brunt of the Union assaults during the morning phase of the Battle of Antietam.

View of Harpers Ferry looking down from Maryland Heights.

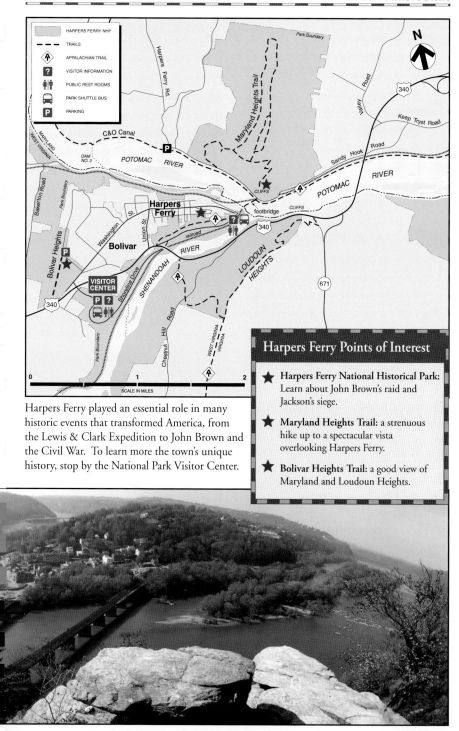

Harpers Ferry played an essential role in many historic events that transformed America, from the Lewis & Clark Expedition to John Brown and the Civil War. To learn more the town's unique history, stop by the National Park Visitor Center.

Harpers Ferry Points of Interest

★ **Harpers Ferry National Historical Park:** Learn about John Brown's raid and Jackson's siege.

★ **Maryland Heights Trail:** a strenuous hike up to a spectacular vista overlooking Harpers Ferry.

★ **Bolivar Heights Trail:** a good view of Maryland and Loudoun Heights.

8 Boonsboro

Site of General Lee's headquarters during the Battle of South Mountain

9 Keedysville

This small town became a vast hospital for wounded soldiers after the Battle of Antietam.

10 Pry House

Site of McClellan's headquarters during the Battle of Antietam. Check with the National Park Visitor Center before visiting this site.

11 Sharpsburg

Founded in July, 1763, the village of Sharpsburg was almost 100 years old and home to approximately thirteen hundred residents at the time of the battle. The photograph below, taken shortly after the battle, depicts Main Street running south west through the village. On the horizon is the location of General Lee's headquarters during the battle.

12 Antietam National Battlefield

Visitor Center Hours: Open Daily
8:30 to 5:00 - September through May
8:30 to 6:00 - June through August

Battlefield Fee: $6 per family or $4 per person - valid for 3 days

Phone: (301) 432-5124

Closed: Thanksgiving, Christmas, New Years

Points of Interest After Antietam

★ **Grove Farm:** Site where President Lincoln visited General McClellan.

★ **Boteler's Ford (C&O Canal NHP):** Site where Lee's army crossed back into Virginia.

★ **Battle of Shepherdstown:** Lee's army fought a rear guard action here on September 19-20, 1862.

General Lee's headquarters

COMPUTER DVD-ROM

THE MODERN WAY TO EXPERIENCE THE HISTORY OF ANTIETAM

 **6 Multimedia Modules**

THE BATTLE MODULE

Experience the Battle of Antietam from an extraordinary birds-eye perspective. For the first time, the events of September 17, 1862, have been reconstructed with computer technology to give you an unparalleled animated picture of this historic battle.

Troop movement animations show you the ebb and flow of the battle

Beautifully illustrated battle maps show historic terrain, buildings and roads

Sound effects, music and musket smoke shock the battle to life!

View the entire battlefield or zoom in for a close-up perspective

Famous battlefield landmarks like Miller's Cornfield and the Dunker Church

Detailed troop movements down to the regimental level

VCR-like controls let you play, pause, rewind and fast forward

1

With the click of a button you can overlay the modern driving tour route onto the historic battle map

Choose from numerous locations or times of the battle to view

Famous historic photographs and beautiful modern day images let you compare the past with the present

Hear what it was like to fight at Antietam from the soldiers who fought the battle. Audio recordings, made from the diaries of soldiers, give you an extraordinary perspective of the struggle.

360° Take a Virtual Tour of the Battlefield

Experience the full grandeur of touring the battlefield of Antietam with over 35 QTVR panoramas of the Antietam National Battlefield and surrounding Maryland Civil War Trail landmarks.

Use your mouse to look in all directions

Explore the Cornfield, Bloody Lane, and other famous sites

Antietam Battlefield Ranger, Keith Snyder, provides an informative background narrative at several critical sites on the virtual battlefield tour.

THE MOVIE MODULE

The 35-minute animated movie is the perfect place to start your Antietam Expedition. It covers the history leading up to and including the battle, giving you a solid foundation to understand the historical context and significance of Antietam.

Learn about the events that launched the campaign

Witness the critical events that shaped Lee's invasion of the North

Watch a high-level overview of the battle

THE ARMIES MODULE

The Armies Module is the perfect place to learn about the commands of Lee and McClellan. Short animated movies describe each army and their dispositions on the eve of the Battle of Antietam. If you are new to the subject, there's a movie that describes how a Civil War army was organized. For the Civil War buffs, there's a detailed order of battle with pictures of the commanders.

Movie describing the Army of the Potomac

Movie describing the Army of Northern Virginia

Movie describing how Civil War armies were organized

THE QUIZ MODULE

Play against another person or the computer. This fun quiz game will let you find out how much you really know about the Battle of Antietam.

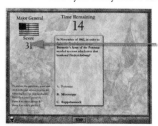

The faster you answer, the more points you score!

Go head-to-head with a friend or solo against the computer

COMPUTER DVD-ROM

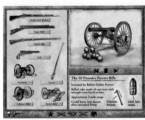

THE WEAPONS & TACTICS MODULE

The Weapons & Tactics Module explains the fighting methods used by generals and soldiers during the Civil War. It also includes a 3D museum that highlights some of the most common weapons used during the period.

A 3D weapons museum lets you explore the weapons up close

Animated movies describe the infantry, cavalry and artillery during the war

The tactics movie explains the changing nature of warfare and its effect on the Civil War

THE TRAVEL INFORMATION MODULE

This module contains the essential information and web sites you need to plan your trip to the battlefield.

Join the TravelBrains Expedition Club

Become a member of the TravelBrains Expedition Club and receive exclusive discounts and new product updates. It's FREE. Join today at: www.TravelBrains.com/club

DVD-ROM Minimum System Requirements

PC minimum system requirements
OS: Windows XP, Vista or later
CPU: Pentium II 233 MHz processor or 100% compatible
Memory: 520 Mb RAM
Hard Disk Space: 50 Mb free hard drive space (uncompressed)
DVD-ROM Speed: 8x DVD-ROM drive
Video card: Capable of 16 bit color at 800x600 resolution
                 Requires QuickTime 3.0 or greater (QuickTime™ 6.0 included)
Sound card: 100% Windows 95/98/2000/Me/XP compatible
Other: 100% Windows 95/98/2000/Me/XP compatible mouse

Mac minimum system requirements
OS: Mac OS 10.0 or later
CPU: Power Mac G3 300
Memory: 520 Mb RAM
Hard Disk Space: 50 Mb free hard drive space (uncompressed)
DVD-ROM Speed: 8x DVD-ROM drive
Video Card: Capable of 16 bit color at 800x600 resolution
                 Requires QuickTime 3.0 or higher